www.rachelshapes.com

Little You

Rachel Nwokoro

Burning Eye

Burning Eye Books
Never Knowingly
Mainstream

This edition published by Burning Eye Books 2019

www.burningeye.co.uk

@burningeyebooks

Burning Eye Books

15 West Hill, Portishead, BS20 6LG

ISBN 978-1-911570-64-6

Little You

Mum and Dad.
You gave me life.
Then
you saved it.
This is for you.

CONTENTS

LOVE

MENTAL HEALTH

This is Little Me:

INTRODUCTION

Hello.

Welcome to my book.

This photo is from my first day of school, playing 'kitchen' with a boy called Andrew. I was about four years old, which, if I can remember rightly, meant I was old enough to terrify my family but young enough not to be expected to know better… a great age.

As I've grown, I've become aware that I've spent a lot of my life standing strong while unconsciously smothering a quiet but honest voice. Life inevitably got busier than it was when I was four, and eventually it became difficult to hear that voice at all. Without much grounding, when the world's seemingly insurmountable demands feel big enough to swallow me whole, I can struggle, as sometimes you might, to access love for myself.

At those times, it helps me to think of Little Rachel.

This baby girl is the little voice I am trying to find again. I feel this immovable duty of care for her. She is small and delicate and has torn through heaven and earth to get me to today. She has fought with death and survived it so now we can share some of our story. She's done her best to keep me here and she is tired.

I owe her
because if I fly
it's because she has been my kitestrings.

Thank you, little one.

I'm listening.

P.S. The business bits are at the back if you're into that.
@RachelShapes

HOW MUCH?

for the attention
of the gentleman
that approached me
and asked

how much?

I am sorry
that I felt the need for some clarification
but you see
in this consumer nation
you would surely appreciate the confusion

stupidly

I was under the illusion
that I looked like a human being
and not a fucking shop

but since you were asking
I would quite like to know
were you wanting some weed or a bag of snow?
or did you think I was dealing in pirate DVDs
because I confess
my cousin still has my copy of *Finding Dory*

but good sir
I do aim to please
so though I can't offer you any of these
I wonder if you could please appease me
and tell me what piece of me
you need

should I be grateful that you asked instead of forcing it on me?
considered presenting it to me
consensually
even offered to pay a fee

oh and what is the going rate for spitting on my civil liberties?

if you let me know
I'll try to sort a *buy one get one free*

I am curious
truly
what it was about me
that made you want to
reduce me
to a juicy
slab of meat

how does it work?

were you looking for a handjob
or a blowjob?
because either way
you are going to remain
unemployed

I even
I even
I even toyed
with the thought that there was something in my look that day

   it must have been something in the way that you dressed

now that I reassess it
I did hear that duffel coats were the new aphrodisiac
shit
I am a sleazy act
call me a slut
I should have known better
I could be a great trendsetter
and convince myself
that this was not a big deal

*it's not a mountain **my dear***
it's a god damn
molehill

and ladies
don't you know that *sex sells?*
he's merely buying
are you even *trying*
to see it from his point of view?

I mean **damn**
look at you
he's asked for your consent
it's got to be a fucking compliment
right?

except
I can't understand how that can be

                                        right

on that night
I tried to fight
and slapped you on the head before you ran
you shit
and I kicked your motorbike to bits
did fuck-all damage
but I went for it
I screamed at you to

dare to come back for it

despite all that
you still managed to make me feel sick
you still made me feel dirty in my own skin
you still managed to make me feel unsafe
three minutes

from my own bed
so when it's all done and said
these words don't help me sleep at night
they don't stop me from being scared of the sight
of the next pizza guy on a motorbike

a friend called me a fucking superhero
but I'm not
so I'd like to hand in the cloak

> *it doesn't make me brave that I spoke*
> it meant I was tired of being afraid

so Mr Pizza Guy
you may think I'm weak
but I'm still going to speak
I might not be the Hulk
but you won't make me believe that
we
can't
be
incredible

not anymore

so here's the final score

I wish I could eradicate you
your existence makes my brain hurt
but I don't think that'd work
because you're like a stray pube
when you get rid of one and
one
two
three
four
five more come to the funeral

so I am just going to say this straight
if you could stop looking for young women on their way home
that'd be just great

trust me
they're not looking for you

if I'm honest
I was looking for a chicken shish with garlic mayo and a
      drizzle of chilli sauce
and I still bought it
and I ate it
and it was amazing
bit expensive but pretty damn tasty
and to answer your question

it was £5.50

Since this poem was written, I have become a vegetarian. But. It's a
poem. And at the time I really really wanted a chicken shish kebab
with that great garlic mayonnaise they do. So. Yeah.

NWANYI

oburu na unu bu nwannem gi nwanyi

I am a different woman to you

nwanyi in the Igbo language means *woman*
oburu na unu bu nwannem gi nwanyi means *if you are my sisters*

listen
ask
act

oburu na unu bu nwannem gi nwanyi
please act like it

abum nwanyi
I am a woman
I am a black woman
I am a queer black first-generation immigrant woman with
     chronic illness and a low income who has been raped
more than once

aha

it is easy to call things Oppression Olympics
it's easy to roll eyes
duck heads
and dismiss it

> *bin all the despair*
> *I want wordplay and quips*

but I can't find the right words
when I'm losing my grip

and there's blood on the floor

and my firefly mind
has declared civil war

I don't always know how to make it poetic
I'm tired
and sometimes
I just want you to get it

oburu na unu bu nwannem gi nwanyi

this cannot be about being comfortable anymore
and for the love of God it cannot be about attributing blame
or feeling guilt
there's no space for it

at the moment
I write like I fight for my life
because that is what I do
daily
so fuck safe spaces

space dominated with shame that
morphs into stardust
floats into the cosmos
inconsequential dark matter
obscuring the whites of your eyes

so you can't quite see
people fighting on wards
hidden in the shadows of their skin
weeping for their lives

it is not enough

one day
one month a year is not enough
I need you to hear me
I need you to hear me
angry
I have reasons to be this fucking angry
and hear me on my terms

not yours
accept that there are reasons
I cannot always smile
and while drowning in waves of empathy
find my eyes in that velvet sea
beckoning
that it is far better
to resurface and
say that
you   don't   know

listen
ask
act

if you are my sisters
act like it

sisters aren't pretty pussies and holding hands
sisters are fights in the earth
and
when I bleed you bleed
because if nothing else
our blood is the same

please don't march with me
and tell them to call us all
wolves that have been whistled at for the last time

I believe you are fighting
but
our battles are different

there are days I have hated white people

there are days I have hated everyone
growing up with the inability
to see any goodness within me

unless it is strength linked to slavery

I can't always be hopeful
I shouldn't have to be

listen
ask
act

oburu na unu bu nwannem gi nwanyi

PROUD TO BE

I feel like I should say that I'm
proud to be a woman
but I'm not entirely sure what that would mean
it confuses me because
check this
I learnt a new word
and it goes

HETERONORMATIVITY

I just learnt it
but guess what?
it already knew me

and I'm sure that you already knew
but just in case

I'll break it down for you

it meant

boys wore blue

and

girls wore pink

and weren't really supposed to think
unless it was about dishes in the kitchen sink
join in girls
it's delightful
it goes

1 2 3 4
I've got to scrub the kitchen floor
5 6 7 8
darn I just broke a plate

and boys you'll be just fine if you're

tough on the exterior
bulldoze anyone that seems inferior
do not cry about things that make you sad
like that you didn't see your favourite granddad enough
before he died
access denied
Mr Man
upon whom we rely

you are definitely not allowed to cry

denied
                        pride

                                    loud and proud

oh and *proud* now equals well-endowed

I wish I could say I was proud to be a woman
but people keep *forcing me to choose* what that means

        do you define my gender by the shape of my body?
            is it that I was born with a v instead of a p?

help me figure it out
because I'm a bit in doubt
about whether it should really shock
that I don't constantly crave a twelve-inch mega-

LOOK

I didn't choose my configuration downstairs
I was born
the doctor checked
and it was there
I didn't do anything to earn it

proud of *being* a woman?
I mean there are still things that make me angry

like people asking when I'm *finally* going to start a family or
finding it unbelievable alarming
that I'm not desperate for a Prince Charming

but
by that same token
try to understand
that just because a woman is not bra-burning
doesn't mean she's not learning
making a male colleague a cup of tea
doesn't mean I'm backing the patriarchy
or suddenly negate my desire for gender equality
but I happen to know that he likes two sugars not three
and I offered
so please stop judging me

I'm not saying I'm *not* proud to be a woman
I just need to redefine what that means
to me
or not define at all
because language can be powerful
but also cruel
and kind of restrictive
not entirely depictive
of the fact that we're all mind-blowingly different

where would the fun be if we were the same?

I see this beautifully weird picture
and I just want to get rid of the frame
because it's old-fashioned
and dull
and made by people who don't know that
colouring out of the lines
can be the fucking coolest way to grow

I guess what I *am* proud of

is what we're starting to achieve
people fighting for the growth of mere possibilities
forums like this
where we're all allowed to have a voice
and whether we speak or not
at least we have the freedom of choice

THE SAME WORDS

so I wanted to try to write a poem
about a word
that no one really wants to hear
I had been tackling it for years
and *then* I realised why I was struggling

do you know what the first thing
I thought was?

how to be

original

like I'm trying to sell a chalkboard
to a five-year-old
with an iPad
and my knees buckle
I'm scared that if I say the word
three out of four heads might drop to the floor
as if we already know the score
Jesus Rachel don't be a bore
not another *rape* poem

I've had a look online and
yeah
there are a lot
more than I'd like to count
it's terrifying the amount
of people it takes to write

and write

and cry

and shout
and each voice is different but all I hear is the same thing

don't rape

so I'm sorry in advance for dropping the word
I know in general it makes people uncomfortable
but

I'm uncomfortable

people are screaming but the world is not listening
I buy the paper and the headline reads

36 women are raped every day

what part of that is in any way okay?
sexual assault in the UK is at an all-time high
yet overall offending is at an all-time low
I've seen the charts and I've read the statistics
but I'm telling you numbers mean nothing
unless you've lived it

take note
crime figures don't mean a lick to the individual

so if you think these words are tired or jaded
look to the woman
whose self-worth has faded
because she truly believes that unless she'd fought to the death
and lost
she'd never be satisfied with how loud her **NO**s were

no matter how *Robin Thicke* you are
the lines are not blurred
a no is a no whether it's drunken or slurred
or screamed or cried
or whispered terrified
in a bedroom between a woman and her wife
it's still rape

and I know what it is to be young these days
rape jokes are on the tip of the tongue
of people who are afraid
to not participate in what the lads call *banter*
lads
it is not banter

85,000 women raped a year is not banter
it's not fair game
and I don't understand how it can be
just a joke
if not everyone is laughing
if more than half the population is crying
and your jokes perpetuate their silence
and make a mockery of the word *consent*

and when the courts are asking questions like

> *how short was your skirt?*
> *how much had you drunk?*

it illuminates the stubborn ignorance in the system
it spits on the face of every goddamn victim
no not victim
survivor
and tells them that they asked for it
I mean am I stupid to think that
the words *rape* and *culture* should not go together?

and before you dare to think it
I'm not man-bashing
I have a father
brothers and men
who I love
and have loved
who would never dare to hurt a woman
a man
a human
and some of whom have been hurt themselves
because yes
men get raped too
but apparently *the figures are lower*
take note

crime figures don't mean a lick to the individual

that's 12,000 men a year too many
being ignored
I abhor the fact that
boys grow up feeling that they can't speak out or they'll be
    seen as

less of a man

I just
I'm running out of words
trying to find an *original* way to communicate
the same fucking words

this is all I have got

don't rape

HOW TO MAKE A MURDERER

he cried

I finished work in Charing Cross
an event management job
the smallest amount of power
to go to anyone's head
but it bought me books
I was too ill to read
and cardigans
and I loved the VIP lanyard
and writing on a clipboard
and giving out free drinks tokens to people twice my age
like Santa Claus
but with cheap vodka

                                        you're fine

one night I actually tweeted
#tragic
it was a wonderful fall from magic
I was everything I would have hated
but chose not to

                                        you're fine

we wanted to go to Heaven
which meant tinny music
sticky floors
and gay white men
calling me gorgeous
and *just like Rihanna*
with clicking tongues
that made me feel uneasy
and unwelcome
but the world was empty
and I wanted to dance till I was dizzy

some of us were turned away
there was no room at the inn
for a queer black girl
without a shiny smile

I went to get the 27 bus
but I needed to piss and it took an hour to get back to Mum's
so I found a passage between two buildings
and a doorway
and I did that classy crouch
(if you don't have a penis you can't just whip it out)
and when I was done

                                                            you're fine

he called out to me from the main street
and asked if I was alright
I pulled up my tights
and called out that
of course

I'm fine   you're fine

he got closer

and

I mean
I wasn't fine
I had to go home alone
and it was cold
and I was tired

but I didn't need help
I'm fine
thank you

                                                    darling

I couldn't hear what he was saying

                                            it's alright

his body blocked out the sound
his accent was heavy

                              don't worry darling

his breath was dense

                                      don't cry

his skin was poison

                                   it'll be alright

it already was

it was

the wind holding its breath

it was

dry swallowing death

it was

sweaty bread

it was

rotting wood

it was

moulding marrow

it was

the neverending February

my friends danced dizzy in Heaven

the devil dragged me to Hell

                                        don't cry

he cried
and I met
the only person I could have killed

he tore a gash through my body

                                        don't cry

and poured tar into the opening

and as I crumbled on the floor

                        please don't cry darling

he grasped at my pieces for absolution

                                        no

he begged me

don't cry

that year I lost too much weight
and people told me I was in great shape

                                you're fine

while I spent months
jumping into broken mirrors
because the shards
felt safer than flesh

                                you're fine

we tell ourselves a lot of lies

I remember that summer
when I first told my dear friend Freddie
about that night
and

don't cry

I said

I'm fine

Freds

and I still have a good heart

but

if I could

I would

find a gun

and aim it at his head

I would

hesitate

wait

and pull the trigger once

because

then

I'm fine

I would not be the only one who had died

TIGER LILY

he said that the lily didn't toil

to be
it took nothing

and I asked
how he could possibly know
what it took
to unfurl those arms
and harden
a bubbling gut

sometimes

just

sometimes

men steal the sun
and replace it with a furnace
and ask us why we're burning

he had consumed her colours for pleasure

but the lily
tender
and outraged
still rose
a tiger roaring
through polluted earth in spring

MEDUSA

do you know that
Athena punished Medusa
for being raped by a man
by giving her *snakes* as a crown?
a phallic halo of hate
a way to call
her fresh trauma
a stain
and to bloody a sacred name

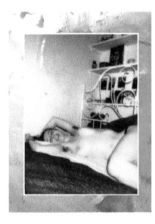

do you know
that there are no
recorded instances of Medusa
turning a woman
into stone?
it's as if she had known
that men might call her
a monster
curse her
banish her into euphemisms
and cyclical rinsing
sheets of unnamed shameful stains

do you know that I call my period Medusa because of you?
and once a month she visits me
usually while I sleep
the old girl's a bit of a creep
and she brings the pain
I tried to sanitise
for years in vain
and brings me pillows
to scream into
with undiluted floods of rage
grieving for the wasted days
I saw myself
as anything less
than a miracle

do you know that she bellows from my core?
validates my backache
warns me not to self-flagellate
instead she says
we should eat biscuits in bed
and find some men with vibrating tongues
and stain their beloved silk sheets
and
come
then come again
vociferously
ejaculate our rage
and soak them with it
soak them with our blood
our clotted
lumpy
smelly
raw
seething
blood
soak them with it
and make them meet
Medusa

MOTHER: SHE LOVED ME

my mother loved me before I was born
years before the hallway lights turned on
she loved me

before she knew me
before that pleasant placenta swelled up
and grew me
wrapped me up in ogbono soup
and yam pounded
by rough brown fists
before she knew sleepless nights like these could exist
she loved me

found me caged in the sky
four miscarriages between
my sister and I
she knew I was waiting
curled up
unabating
she loved me
and love liberates
so she spends her life and mine praying
for her love to set me free

ME TOO

I need to write
a quiet note
to all the humans
who can't find solace in hashtags
who can still barely find the words

friend
you can't join a movement if you *can't move*
some pain remains frozen
regardless of what trends
healing does not heed a time frame

maybe today
the only thing that you can declare
timidly
is that

you're still here

DTMH

when I was little
I hated my mum
for taking her time
to protect my hair
because children told me
that they could see my scalp
and that it was weird
and so I felt ugly
and I wanted to feel beautiful
and I am only now seeing
what the world made
that little girl feel

from time to time
when I see my military styles
answer to a white woman
I want to ask her if she has read
the terms and conditions
what it means to enlist without permission
our soldiers burn our scalps
and we
in turn
protect our land
righteously
by applying shea butter daily
to feed armies
standing in cornrows

we braided the shame
the discovery of fallen hair heroes
in the bottom of my school bag

extradited childhoood

these are not yours
these are not yours
these are not yours

I wonder if there will ever be a story

that the black girl will tell

I REMEMBER

I remember being about seven and this boy called Shane
no
no
Shaun
asking why
my hair looked like spiders
I remember being eight or nine and Niamh making up a game
    that I wasn't allowed to play
and I remember asking over and over and over again why and
    she wouldn't tell me
and she wouldn't look at me
and somehow I knew but I wanted her to say it – which she did
she yelled it

you can't play this game because you're not white!

and I remember running to the teacher and I couldn't
    understand why Niamh was crying so much
and everyone looked very serious
and Niamh begged me not to let the school call her mum
and said she would invite me to her birthday party
and I really really wanted to go because the whole class was
    going
so I said okay and all was forgotten
but in the end
she didn't invite me to her party
and I never got to play the game
and I still wish I knew what it was

I remember being eight and asking my mum to chemically
    straighten my hair
because I never felt pretty
because it wasn't straight
I remember it burning my scalp and being told that the exposed
    flesh and crusting skin was *normal*
and then I remember that week when I came into sixth form
    with an afro and everyone thought it was okay to put their
    dirty hands in my hair

asking *can I touch it?* and not waiting for a response doesn't
    mean you've asked
Kelly
and I know you don't wash your hands as often as you should
Kelly

so please
don't touch my hair

I remember getting all dressed up for a night out in Newcastle
    in the first week of university and getting an egg thrown on
    my face from a car
I remember every time I've been called the word nigger
every   single   time
I remember every look that has said **you don't belong here**
I remember every time I've been the only black girl in the room
I remember every scrunched-up face at my unusual name

who decides what's usual?

I remember when I said nothing because I didn't have a voice
but then I remember finding one and being told I was angry or
    over-sensitive or that it's okay if it's casual

being a cunt part-time still makes you a cunt

and actually maybe I am angry
wouldn't you be?
shouldn't you be?

I remember my baby cousin telling me that her friend told her
    that she was ugly and her friend's mum said she wasn't
    allowed to play with black girls anymore
and I remember every time a guy has told me that he only dates
    chocolate girls and thought it was a compliment
I remember having my hair pulled out and being kicked to the
    floor

I remember when I discovered the blacktag
it's what I call it in my head when a white person kills a black
    person with impunity and social media goes crazy and it
    starts trending like

#SandraBland #EricGarner #MarkDuggan #BlackLivesMatter
yeah but why the hell do we still need reminding?

and I remember being terrified if I ever had a baby boy and his
    name started
trending

I remember every time my skin has felt heavy
I remember the big things and I remember the small things
    that still feel huge

I remember so much
so much more

I remember so much
that I can't forget
and I wish I could

GRAPEFRUIT

I was reared to recognise

[grapefruit-blotched skin]

the cry of a white woman
before my own

some years ago
I found my tears

[dried ink wells]

embedded in the calluses on my feet
growing through the throb in my back
asleep in the dark centre of my fists
sticking to my fingertips
staining overlooked pages
and
after some time
reabsorbed by my skin

my tears were never pretty
but with them
I wrote poetry

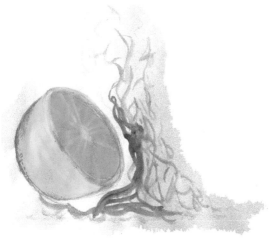

NWAMAKA

nnem
no matter how hard I try
my conditioning means I always feel more
beautiful
when I've ironed out my kinks

nwamaka
curls in your crown are your birthright
handed down by the queens
that fought before you
discover the tender peace
that lives in
starving
your eyes
of beauty
and feeding
your soul
in defiance

MOTHER: LEARNING

I was taught to reject myself at ten
taught to hate my discoloured school uniform and pretend that I
was forced into this skin
the here-there struggle of first-generation immigrants
a mother with no money but extremely overweight bags packed
with pride
I was taught to be embarrassed by her hairnets
her other jobs
her untouchable survival
and she
always
always
forgave me

so I think I owe it to her now
to learn to forgive myself

COLLECTING ROOTS

my natural roots begin to nourish me
travelling to my centre and connecting me to the earth
while pale voices surround me
unground me
unsteady feet search for patches of sun-bathed grass
I grab a dab hand
force my light under a pair of severed tights
fix Astroturf atop my crown
because that's what I do on less confident days
when my defences are deflating
and my solar plexus imploding
and my solar system corroding
I disguise the tracks
and listen to you say that this style is *by far your favourite*
lifeless strands
uprooted from their homes and occupying foreign soil
these lies help you to see that
I am beautiful
and some days
I need that
so my unsteady feet dance to your praise
as I feel the glow in my crown
dim
tired
for lack of use

MAGIC

Dear
Black
Girls,

You
should
love yo-
urself
because
you are
needed & im-
portant in
this w-
orld.

Love Ijeoma

Cashauna.
Chizara.
Precious.
Ebere.
Emma.
Zara.
Moni.
Sade.
Stephanie.
Vogue.
Cartier.
Janet.
Maryam.
Vanessa.
Aimee.
Julie.
Ugonna.
Maya and Trudie.
Yoyo.
Rose.
Chicago.
Camilia.
Tendai.
Caroline.
Kimberley.
Ann.
Lynette.

Heatha.
Ijeoma.

Lauren.
Janet.
Dominique.
Loren.
Paula.
Angel.
Tobi.
Nayyirah.
Kelechi.
Sacha.
Chidera.
Sister.
Tanusha.
Before you died.
Every aunty that came bearing jollof rice.
All of your mothers.
All of mine.

Life is hard but you are here. That is fucking incredible.
Especially because practising self-love in the world as it is has
become radical activism.
It is political warfare to say *fuck you, adverts*.

I love myself.

And every day I see Black Women on the battlefield, struggling
against a society that feeds on their perceived inadequacy and
refusing to believe that their mere existence

is

extraordinary.

Refusing to believe that their magic lies not in

what   they   do

but in

that   they   live.

Exist loudly, sisters.

Our stories deserve to be told.

I will film that bike montage

And

Make them eat it.

We are dangerous and tender.

We
Are
Here.

Writing a book is tricky. To be clear, I do not subscribe to an idea of political blackness. This poem is first and foremost for black women. To me, black means of African or Caribbean heritage. But some of the women in this list are women of colour that I believe also deserve all the claps and I'm not about to write a whole 'nother poem, so… it's my book and here we are.

I am magical
because I understand
how to love myself
and others. ♥

Ijeoma
Age: 10

MOTHER: EATING OUT WITH MY AFRICAN MOTHER

I bought you lunch today
laughed when you said that the meal was great but
you *definitely* could have made it yourself at home
and watched
you lost
love and peshwari on your palate
a three-course meal
ending in cinnamon ice cream
that we'd never been able to afford
and still can't

but I am old enough to make the decisions now
and you're old enough to let me

> *let's just leave without paying*
> *what can they do?*

Mum
you refuse to walk fifteen minutes without saying

> *let's get the bus*
> *have you forgotten I am a pensioner?*

in your old age and on a rampage
so sorry to break it to you
but we absolutely will not be planning
any quick getaways

small-nosed
gap-teethed
tongue-waggled

reflection of me

you act all polite and painfully white when the waitress comes
over

the perfect display of what eating lunch out might look like

and I fall in love with you

at the station you look up and frown
sceptical that the Central line can still take us home
because you are sure this isn't the station that we came from

and I remember
that when I was little and I stopped
uncertain
you would just take my hand tight
and gently pull me in the right direction

my guide

uncertain on the Underground
now I grab onto yours

it's my turn

FREE LABOUR

I manage to convince myself that
I have found peace with my reality
until I willingly fall into a
below-the-surface
that is
subglacial basic
conversation
(and I rarely do)
with a straight white man

it hampers my breathing
centuries of bloodshed
press down on my lungs
I fight with my tongue
retching facts and dispelling theories
that he read on Buzzfeed that one time
about how race is a social contruct
and well
                    it's all a matter of perspective you see?

and I really want to believe
that Chester is trying to fuck with me
so I can finish my Jameson
wash my face
and go to bed
but instead

I wait

and
earnest eyes
provoke me
every time
I need to crumble his denial
with dark streets
and ripped tights
and hate spat as I hold her hand at night

disowned children
an empty fridge
you mention your friend born in Kenya
as if I'll know who the fuck she is

how at acting auditions
multilingual English actually means **street**
and *street* means **black**
and *black* means **me**

jumping over train barriers
when I couldn't afford the fare

can you see my legs are broken
as you pass me on the stairs?

hurdles became a given
and I *hate* that I want you to care

you stepped on my hands
refused to understand
furrowed your brow
shook your head
then said

> *life is what we make it darling*
> *everyone struggles my pet*

and I can see I have spent these hours
running to you
while you've sat in your Fiat 500 with the radio on
humming to a different tune
and watching me
still running
and I decide
to stop running

teach yourself

I am tired

I know it's hard for all of us
but
you have power
and I don't
and it kills me

you have to do something

do something

BE MORE DOG

I was walking down the road the other day

well it wasn't actually the other day it was a few years ago
now but when I'm writing I feel like I've got to say everything
happened *when I was walking down the road the other day* like in
a comedy routine maybe so that what I'm saying feels relevant
and relatable and **now** and therefore must be more important
when it really actually happened two years ago

but for all intents and poetry purposes

I was walking down the road *the other day*
when I read the sign from a popular advertising campaign for
    a phone shop that said

BE
MORE
DOG

no

I might be more *cat*
or meerkat
or more marmoset
or more of an animal neither of us has discovered yet

but I will not

be
more
dog

so to clarify

I should be skinnier
but curvier
lighter
no

whiter
straighter
self-hater
and shameful masturbator
equal parts better at sex
but with an innocence complex
up-to-date with the latest fashions
but with £2 a month's worth of charitable compassion
and now you want me to

be   more   dog

I was walking in Finchley Road
the other day

when I passed another advert that read

IT'S NOT A SOFA IT'S A CONCEPT

ok
cool

it's just
it looked just like
a sofa
so
can I ask
what exactly
is
this concept?
and this *concept*
this not-a-sofa *concept*

how was it conceived?
can I be part of the conception?

because if I could
I think I'd choose one with some wear and tear
can it smell like fart
and Netflix marathons
and whenever I cry because I feel completely alone
and whenever I cry because I realise I'm not
I want it to have burns in it
from those cigarettes
when I laugh so much
I forget to ash

I want it to hold my niece's bad dream piss
and the stillness of the time my mum held me in complete
        silence for an hour
because she had no words to change things but
damn it she would if she could

can it blow bubbles that are just the right size to pop so you
        don't get soaked?
can it feed me chocolate that doesn't make me feel ill-equipped
        for the beach?
and the glass of wine that didn't make it all their fault?
and the can of Diet Coke that doesn't inexplicably make me
        want to fuck the gardener?
and a massage because it feels good
not because I'm getting older?
and oh
can it also

be
more
fucking
dog

because if it can't then

that's okay
I think it'd be unreasonable to
expect all that
it can just be a sofa
it can just
be

GLITTERY SLUDGE

to those who don't understand festivals
an introduction:

I fell asleep in a gummy bear tent
and woke up on the moon
squelching through
glittery sludge
biodegradable trenches
and Rhian's piss
delicately drips
into grass built like glowing green stars

a field full of impossibilities
ludicrous synchronicities

it's how I know there's such a thing as magic
but I hate the graveyard of leftover plastic
I wish our warm vibrations took better care of the planet

a family of lost souls
closed eyes swaying
goddesses playing
three-note melodies into hidden chambers
found in forests filled with
kaleidoscopic lights
love-tinted glasses
a kingdom of storytellers
a community of kindness
misty mornings on blow-up mattresses
every path a greeting
every smile a compass

drained batteries
and full hearts

a escape into belonging
iridescent scatter

and for four solid days
the world being fucked
didn't matter

and I'm driving away from my imagination
in an overcrowded coach heading back to civilisation
and the engine sounds like a deep house track
and there's a bottle of Bombay Sapphire
from the family before
and all I can think is
how grateful
how very very grateful I was
to be here

GREEN TEA IN THE WHEELHOUSE

Linda wants me to pinpoint
when exactly
we might have lost the flag
right nasty old rag but you'd be surprised
what people will do
to show they know where they've set sail from

you can't capture flags in a panoramic view
refusing to halt for pixels
while crystals cutting midnight cream
purple skies
confide that the novelty of mushrooms on moorings
can ebb away after a twelve-hour shift
and seven charity appeals

do we design buildings the way we do for structural integrity?
is this a tried and tested model?
because it isn't very inventive
squares and rectangles
and clumsy cable cars carrying ghosts

I want to see a trapezium
some squiggly lines
instead of intercontinental mirrors
and clinking glasses of champagne
reflecting my own disconnect
and a river with many faces

some: magic
most: mundane

grime
climbs
up
walls
like
it

misses
the
forest

earnest cranes frame the city
scraping the skies
with luminescent arms
which is obscene because
there clearly isn't enough space for them all
reaching
for
something

                                    n
                                  i
                                a
                              t
                            r
                          e
                        c
                      n
                    u

and I think
I know the feeling

island gardens
grow over Scrap Iron Park
spend millions to replace an old scrap yard with lovely
pagodas
regenerate
regenerate
regenerate
scrap metal
until unrecognisable
and sell them 'West Greenwich'
at twice the price
because it sounds better than Deptford

but it's still Deptford

thirty years of rising tides
and it's still Deptford

this water is dense
stolen utterances need time
let them sink in
let them sink
one sink is
filling itself to the brim with dirty dishes
Fairy liquid and secrets

an abundant body
impenetrable
but by these watermen

and when I see clouded faces
the same colour as these waters
I thrust my hand into their depths
unpick the absorbed burdens
that do not belong there
decontaminate and distil
so that all that lives can breathe
gentle air

godspeed
endeavour
and hope of a safe return
no one will ask why I'm here
I still have so much to learn

is the city aware of the importance of sleep?
it's midnight and all the lights are still on
that's not a great before-bedtime routine

but Dave A the skipper says
when he first came afloat
the commercial side of the river was dying
bleak

derelict
and when parties like this were done
the river was pitch black because there wasn't a soul

and I furrow my brow because I can't see how there could be
     more soul here now
than there was then

Dave A
offers me a drink
Jim stifles a smile
because I ask for green tea
please

and I'm not sure that's really a waterman's drink
but Jim is kind and really I think he just enjoys saying the
words
green tea
in the wheelhouse

gliding on the Thames feels like
flight
welcoming bubbles
and gulls
silent gulls searching for mini industrial beaches
greyed sand melts around a bald man searching for treasure
unquestioned
waiting

we pass by

Dave A tells me the origin of the word *toerag*
and I feel warm despite the wind

community is tempting
even when it floats

please have a safe journey home

LITTLE WISHES

- I wish arcades would turn their lights off when they are empty
- I wish people didn't barter with sex workers
- I wish she was still alive
- …or I wish I had said goodbye
- I wish GPs weren't writing prescriptions for food
- I wish I could build a home in your lips
- I wish I could bask in the sun like a little lizard
- I wish London felt less fast
- I wish for peace for black women
- I wish you'd listened to me
- I wish those ten years of us had been different
- I wish oat milk was available at all coffee outlets
- I wish you hadn't taken your hurt out on me
- I wish you hadn't been hurt at all
- I wish people who ask themselves rhetorical questions and then immediately answer them… would stop. E.g.: Did I start this list without knowing where it was going? Absolutely. Do I regret it? Perhaps.
- I wish I didn't live in the past and future
- I wish I spoke French fluently
- I wish you hadn't asked me to lie
- I wish 'Tea for the Tillerman' was a longer song
- I wish I had been kinder to myself

THE PINK DRESS

In 1972 or thereabouts, my dad moved to England because he wanted a better life. In 1975, my mother followed suit. Except that she moved to England for a different reason. To put it simply, three years previously, she'd stupidly fallen in love. The things we do for a heart that still beats.

My mum stepped off the plane, she told me, and she was scared.

> *Ijeoma,*
> *she whispered.*
> *Safe journey.*

She said she'd never felt so cold. But she was wearing a pink dress and it was the seventies and she wanted the things she'd dreamt of when she and her seven siblings fought over the last piece of meat in the bottom of the egwusi soup pot. She stepped off that plane holding a suitcase with dreams bursting from the seams and wearing a pink dress with flowers on that didn't quite fit right but made her think that she might be happier one day. And she doesn't know if she's ever seen her breath in front of her face like that. So she holds it. Because she doesn't like the way it looks like a ghost. And for a moment the only reason she knows she's still there is because she puts her hand to her chest and feels that she's got a heart that still beats.

They talk about the American dream, but my mum had an English one. It sounded pretty nice, to be fair. It didn't really sound like she wanted to take over the country or demand rights she didn't deserve or burn the Union Jack, or steal jobs from babies or John or whoever it's meant to be or rape our women and our men at the same time or generally make the place look untidy. It didn't ring in my ears like that, her dream. No, my mum's was modest. I reckon, anyway. She wanted to learn. She wanted to learn like she couldn't back home and she wanted to not have to go to the bathroom in the dark. She wanted a family that she could look after and love and that didn't have to suffer like she had and would.

But my mum and dad didn't get to live their dreams, so I am

grateful to get to live mine. They worked more jobs than they care to recount in the stories they tell me, squeezed tight into the smallest beds with a baby on each knee and a book in each hand. They fought for admission to study and, God, did they study hard. And they'd miss meals so their children wouldn't. They felt how it hurt to be weak so their children could grow knowing the value of strength.

Strength they *had* to learn to protect little hearts that beat.

I mean, we've all closed our eyes and drifted to somewhere better. Somewhere with colours that hurt a little less on the eyes and soul. So that isn't an immigrant thing, dreaming; it's a human thing, right? We all do it.

My parents are British citizens. But they know they don't belong there. I was born there, but people tell me to *go home.* But that doesn't matter. It doesn't matter because when they say *go home*, my mum closes her eyes and smiles in that way she does and says that one day, my friend, she will.

But then, these people that we see, on the news and on TV – these people that aren't standing outside a plane in a pink dress with white flowers on that means that one day they might be happier, but are running, swimming, bleeding and screaming their way to survival – can't dream of going home when people tell them to. They can't go home. And every new door they try to walk through gets slammed, shut and bolted.

And all I can see is pictures of them holding their heads so tight to each other's chests. And I think, you know what, I don't blame them for checking. If I were them, I'd be listening too.

Because the world won't stop failing to hear that their hearts still beat.

A LETTER TO FAITH

Dear Faith,

I've been meaning to write a letter to you for a while but I haven't known what to say. My earliest encounter with you was at the dinner table when Dad blessed dinner.

In Jesus' name we pray, amen.

You glowed white and filled the pews at church every Sunday. I saw you when my mum closed her eyes and held her hands upwards. You never spoke to me much then, Faith. So I coloured pictures on my hands and knees while Mum asked me to press my hands together and say what I'm thankful for.

I was thankful for crayons.

I met you a little later, though, by myself. You glimmered with a blue haze and found me crying at four in the morning. I spent my teen years bent over a socket. Turning it on and off because one, two, three, four. Not safe. Hand gel in one hand and tissues in the other. Afraid to touch anything in case it made my sister's neck break. You held me in the early hours and made me believe that I wasn't alone.

Then I remember the years that I lost you. I wish you hadn't left. Those years were cold. I looked for meaning in the dusty remnants of our vacuum cleaner. Furious at you. I felt the hot coal singeing my hand but somehow expected you to feel the pain. You weren't with me then. So I let go of the anger and I let go of the coal. Those years were important. But I wouldn't repeat them.

Let's change direction.

Faith, I remember when I first slept with a woman. Two freshers at university, dressed as Oompa Loompas on a netball social. Kissing in the smoking area of a club which, in 1996, was unashamedly crowned *the second worst nightclub in Europe* by FHM.

We squashed into the corner with coy smiles and smelling like Jaeger, shaking with the excitement of leaving footprints in untouched soil.

The clock struck three and 'That's Amore' blasting through the speakers signalled it was time to leave. She came back to mine that night and it was the first time I'd kissed a girl who had made me hope for something more.

Hope is a dangerous mistress, Faith.

I wish you'd warned me about her.

Next morning, purple bra strewn on the floor and there you were, Faith. Back in my life. But this time searing red rays behind my eyes. Banging the words

shame, guilt, sin, wrong

around my head like a song whose lyrics I wanted to forget, and it confused my naïve and defiantly liberal younger self. I asked her to leave. Made jokes to my friends that I'd had a **'proper mental night woke up with this girl half naked in my bed WAHEY WHAT THE HELL AM I LIIIIIKE?'** and spent the rest of the year being called the college dyke. And laughing. On the outside. But silent and terrified everywhere that counted.

I apologised to her years after, don't worry. When I found my feet again. But university netball training had never been the same after that. I wish the fear of being judged hadn't made me avoid everyone's eyes so much.

I knew it made her feel bad.

Now, I'm a little older and have flicked the dust out of my eyes and I see you in the most unlikely of places. You definitely get around. You surround me from time to time and pop little purple fireworks as I walk. I clawed my way out of an existence without you and realised that I just didn't like being told how to see you.

So, yes, now I'm a little older and I think you glow purple.

I see you in people. I see you in poetry. I see you in frozen moments. In waterfalls in December. I see you in the sky at night and, for the first time in my life, I see you in myself. I never thought I'd be able to write a letter to you, Faith, and say the things I'm saying now.

But now I feel like I'm learning to trust and be okay with who I am and understand that maybe I don't need to fight so much. You glow purple in this room, Faith, and let me trust that there are a few spaces with people who want to help you feel strong enough to speak.

This is the first letter I'm writing to you, Faith, but I doubt it'll be the last.

Thank you for being part of my journey, when you could be. Thank you for giving me space when you couldn't.

I'll see you about.

Love,

Rachel

OASIS AND VAPORUB

so here I am
trying to start

a revolution from my bed

at this point
I've got a blank Google Doc entitled
The Revolution
and a runny nose

I'm looking back at you in anger
because you made this sound easy

CHANGE

This is a call and response poem, but if you're reading it in a book then we can't really do that bit because I'm probably not in the room with you. Or am I under the bed?

No, I'm not, that would be inappropriate.

*Whenever you see the word **'CHANGE'**, I'd really like it if you would close your eyes, say the word to yourself, breathe and then keep reading.*

Thank you.

I'm screaming and I don't want to
maybe you're angry too
I can't hear you but that's okay
just scream a little louder

I know it's on the inside
that's okay too
I'm doing this for me
and you
if you're there

I am shouting at the top of my lungs and I really don't want to
I've been told frequently
that as a professional voice user
screaming is decidedly bad for my vocal cords
but I'm still doing this
for me
and you
if you're there

vocal cords are these little flaps in our throats that look like
     aliens
in case you didn't know
because I didn't know before I went to a speech and
     language therapist called Jenny
every week
she's got a manic smile
she's too stern with me and I don't like it
and her hair is stupid

mine are bumpy because I smoked too much as a teenager
and because my family never learnt how to listen to each
other so everyone grew up shouting to be heard
that's why I wake up some mornings and sound like a car
exhaust pipe for no reason
at all
bumpy
my vocal cords
not Jenny
she was not bumpy

I'm shouting and I don't want to
I don't want to shout
so I'm going to stop now

and I don't know how to write poems anymore

CHANGE

I think I write poetry in order to communicate
but I'm brassic if you ask me to communicate how not to hate

my pockets are empty
I'm dirt poor for ammunition
even if I had some
it'd be ill-sufficient for this mission
my weapon is my voice
and it's getting hoarser by the day
I don't speak as loud anymore
because I'm running out of things to say

and from experience it's a concept that the universe will not
take
because I'm seeing quadruple negatives
so I'd prefer a little release
instead of speaking on anti-hate
I want to switch to pro-peace

CHANGE

when I wrote this
I felt compelled to communicate some sort of message of hope
but sometimes all I've got is the truth
and that is that I'm fucking struggling to cope
you're not supposed to say that when you perform
you're supposed to have it all together
but thing is I'm out here holding on to my last tether
so don't think that I am clever because I can string together
a rhyme
this poem is like a feather
it'll have no direction
          only time
              spent
                and a
                    gentle
                        swaying
                            descent

CHANGE

when I lost my best girl at twenty-two I realised she sought
    peace so much
she needed to rest
in
it
I didn't get it at the time but I guess the logic fits
in a society that continually fails sufferers of mental health
the biggest battle can be to fall asleep and wake up not hating
    yourself

CHANGE

I'm so easily distracted
darkness cannot destroy darkness
heavy aching wounds
straining backs

cut-off wings
and broken tracks

CHANGE

track record
he had a track record
he had a track record of selling CDs
he had a track record of selling cigarettes
he had nasty track record of inhaling and exhaling while black
now he has a death certificate

CHANGE

right
fuck hate
let's start to educate because
bigotry is learned
privilege is not earned
and I'm not playing the race card
I simply wasn't dealt that many other ones
so I just want to talk to whoever's fixing the game
and demand that they take out the jokers
because this shit's not funny anymore

CHANGE

I smell the blood of my brothers and sisters falling in the
streets
and I'd be lying if I said it didn't make me feel weak
at the knees

CHANGE

maybe this one's broken
broken tracks
but I don't want to fight back
I wanna throw the record player at the wall and say

HELLO WORLD

and bring together an orchestra of unlikely souls
and teach them to tapdance a beat that hasn't been invented yet
and I want to close my eyes and listen
and turn that rhythm into poetry

because my tracks are broken
my words already spoken
and jaded
and I can't make this palatable
I'm not indefatigable

I tire easily

CHANGE

**they say that people shout when they're angry because their
hearts get far apart**

did you know that?
to cover the distance they've got to scream to be able to hear
each other

by that logic
the angrier they are
the louder they have to shout to hear each other over the
distance of their hearts
and
you see
I am tired of shouting
I don't want to shout

they say that people shout when they're angry because their
hearts get far apart

and when we fall in love
we speak softly

because then
our hearts are so close
that every single decibel
reverberates
for an infinity
and my love

we don't need that many

so in theory
I'm fighting to get my heart so close to this world
I don't need to say a word

you know those times when you've loved so much that you
    look into each other's eyes and say nothing
but you can feel every single word
even the naughty ones
especially the naughty ones

I'm tired of speaking
I want to say nothing
and know that my heart is close to yours
speak softly
and then say nothing
I want to fall in love with the world
and say nothing

CHANGE

SNAP ELECTION

ike na kwusie ike
fuerte y estable
fort et stable
strong and stable

change must be gradual
is constantly chimed
but surely we are
out of time
and out of clocks

as the dreaded date draws forward
tick searches for the tock

young warriors
must unlearn that
our votes
are merely
lost lines in a box

they are lines
yes it's true
but instead
in never-ending queues
for broken banks
where scraps of food
are a currency
that nurses cannot afford

straining to nourish themselves
and our children
with a tablespoonful of reform

built on a forsaken NHS
and rejected application forms
my friends
silence
is crippling the poor

but what's the point in voting?
'cause nothing changes right?

every young person I speak to
feels unheard in this fight

but if revolutionaries before us
had thought the very same
I'd have no vote and many of us
would currently be in chains

how can we make a call to action
if our inaction means
we cannot afford our phones
and the numbers of those
we did not preserve
dissolved
to dial tones?

silence is no longer a privilege
if it leads to slow and tormenting death

so I am begging you
take your frustration and
fury
and take a goddamn pen

ask for help to vote by proxy
post
or feel it out in braille
wheel up the ramps
before
they're gone
and we must battle to

SAVE OUR HAND RAILS

I don't care which way you vote

it is your right to choose
but if we don't
at least
show up
then
all of us will lose

BLACK BOXES WHERE THEY DO NOT BELONG

standing outside North Kensington Methodist Church
Sister asks where I live and I look down
say ten minutes away
on my bike

weathered fingers
defiant grasp
clasping onto the Virgin Mary
bent over a cross
and no one knew where Jesus was

two faded faces in her cotton creases

thank you for coming
I've worked all over the world
and everyone in this community has been so kind
so kind
my two carers are in heaven now
PRAY FOR US
WE NEED YOUR PRAYERS

holding a young woman I'd never met
kissing the hair huddled in her neck
her head made to take respite on my forearm scars
I want to
t h i c k e n my branches
and wrap them around her
forge myself out of *stronger* stuff

my skin should turn
to oak that must never burn

that must **never** burn
that must burn
never
that
burn that

oak that must never burn

and for her to smell me reminiscing about how
Tavistock Gardens changes on carnival days
and how she prefers it on Sundays

but I don't know this woman
and I'm holding her for less than forty-seven seconds
and I wonder why I come
because I can't take this grief away
or change its shape

I
keep my eyes on boxes full of kitchen roll and tins and cans
change the stale water of mourning bouquets that refuse to wilt

I want to help
cos we have to do something

keep my eyes on boxes
and avoid the twenty-four-storey box of blackened ash

can you feel it from here?

a monument to the degradation of our society
stacked in broken burned boxes
row on row where they do not belong

and I wonder when Jesus is getting here

because surely he'd be able to explain and account for
hundreds of

denied names
denied burials
denied grief

he will account for them when he has ink in his pen
and time to think

my mother never taught me how to hate
insisted I missed school that day
etched peace into my veins
and love in the label of my uniform so I didn't forget

Mary is bent over the cross and Jesus hasn't shown

my mother never taught me how to hate
so I skipped the tests
because I knew I'd fail

instead spinning dizzy
drinking chemical-blue WKD
tipsy
when I should have been in the *library*
like I said I was
studying how to

       cull *suppress* cull *s u p p r e s s* cull *suppress*

use

rage

to fuel this revolution

spit love in their faces
watch them gag
and ask them
what the hell they were expecting

I brought that statue to Mum

the one where Jesus had gone
she's a big fan
and I wondered if she knew where he'd got to

she said

    he'd asked his mother to have his back

his hands weren't quite ready to carry it
wounds hadn't yet healed
and he couldn't fill out the forms
and they wouldn't give him the support

and mothers are supposed to be at good that

I thank the universe
say **I know what I have**
and the *moment* I forget

I'll look for my mother.

Rest in peace to the victims of Grenfell Tower.
Unending love and support to the survivors.
You deserve more.

HOW TO BE AN ALLY

Ava

I am sorry that that's happened. I'm sorry that our industry continues to do two dimensional 'inclusive diversity' or whatever the fuck they call it without any actual effort or resources put in to championing, inspiring and encouraging B.A.M.E artists/creators/producers. I am sorry that white people continue to take and take and take. I can never know what that robbery feels like but I am, unwaveringly, quietly (when I should be) and loudly (when you need me to be) behind you. Not in front, not beside, behind you, following you in to the future you will carve for generations and yourself.

iMessage

MOTHER: EARTH

I ran my fingertips over what she had left us
stalactite lions
potent ripples
and
mothering mountains

I spend my time
looking down
while
picking up
discarded cigarettes
and apologising to the earth

this is our legacy

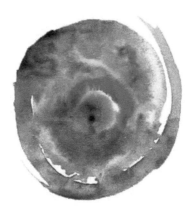

INDEPENDENCE DAY

October waits

demanded recognition
expected jubilation
reluctant creation

forced words
every year
squeezing gratitude
like drops of ripe orange
that you picked
for your children to lick
orange will not feed their hearts
but chop now

chop

you were hungry
your flagpole raped my soil
and a princess pulled it out
and when I go home
that hole remains empty
my brothers harvest around it:
commemoration

Nwokoro means
the son of a strong man

I am the daughter of many strong men
I will not celebrate today
for I cannot be liberated by you

VERTIGO

I know you saw me fall
but I don't know why you say
you didn't

are you protecting me?
or are you shaming yourself
for watching me
reach
such
heights
without a net?

please don't worry
I would do it again

for better or worse
it was the fear
of
nothing
to catch me

that got me there

SOFT LANDING

if I slid out of my skin before the final ten seconds
and fell onto padded ground
would you call that cheating
or can it be allowed because I didn't know
and because the shimmering corners of your heart
made of lights
knew that what I so needed

w
a
s

a

s
o
f
t

l
a
n
d
i
n
g

MY REAL NAME

I learnt to say my name when I was three

> a whisper
> ticked boxes
> and uncertain capitalisation

> discriminate
> medicate
> overcompensate

I am the introduction of a 'fitness to study' policy after a
suicide attempt

> you've made an impact even in your absence

I am absence

> the fabric picked away on an empty chair
> and where's it from?

> was I there?
> was I theirs?
> was I yours?

I am extended apologies

> forced smiles until the creases ache

I am affectionate

> so you will accept my hug
> make an exception
> for this display of affection
> so that no one can claim that you
> treated me differently

I am differently

I am

> awkward phrasing

                                        apprehensive pronunciation

                                                                    how
my
                                                        how would
my
                                                    how would you
my name
                                            how would you prefer to

my name is

                                            could you spell that?

my name is

                    how would you prefer to identify yourself?

my name is

                                    could you just write that down?

my name is

                        Chiedozie Amarachi Rachel Nwokoro

                                    Chiedozie

                                    Amarachi

                                    Rachel

                                    Nwokoro

                I learnt how to say my name when I was three

say my name   say my name

love

OH DEAR

there's all this mounting pressure
from I don't know what
like a balloon filled with loneliness waiting to go

pop

telling me
that I'll burst at the seams
that I have got to find the person of my dreams
in every independent coffee shop
or that balloon will fucking pop

and then I'm left panicking
that if I don't find someone
I'll be left with
me

and surely
that's a fucked-up philosophy

wanting to spend more time with *my cat Milly*
then I do with myself

I want to take a book off the shelf
and read
until the pages are wrinkled
and the evening is sprinkled with a mad sparkle of
contentment
the kind that says
this is great and I'd like to share it

so I do

swipe left
swipe right
praying to God that I just might
come across enough Tinder matches

to ignite
that fire I am terrified will never be there
that spark
that flame
that all-consuming love affair
that I had heard about
from a friend of a friend
who sang in my ear
that

anything is possible if you just believe in love
sorry
love
but I call **bullshit**
now understand that
I'm not a cynic
but it's a four-letter word
I've so often heard
and as much as I've learnt over the years
it's become abundantly clear
I could fit that knowledge on the end of a thumb tack
because the overwhelming fact is that
there isn't a right or a wrong
there are just choices

we just are and it just is

so I meet you
and make sure to say
let's keep it casual
because of course that is what is naturally
in the best interests of both of us
nothing much to discuss

maybe
if we're both clear from the start

we won't need to worry about breaking each other's
hearts
and
we'll keep dancing
because it's *fun*
and we're not hurting anyone
and I'll have no trouble in saying
that you never cease to amaze
when I realise
that you've worn the same jumper for **five days**
then I realise that I only noticed
because I've been there for all five of them

oh dear

ever thought of yourself as the kind of person
that can dismiss feelings at the drop of a hat?
I thought I was really great at that
that I could start something that I knew would come to an end
I'd lean my head to the left
and ask if we could
still be friends?
because I've felt love and it can be fantastic
but there's something to be said for all the other shit
the *this is really just for now schtick*
I thought I was bloody great at it
but then there's that **oh dear**
you know that one from before
when it appears to be clear that you've become my greatest fear

cheers

and when I accidentally say something weird
then I listen when you laugh
a bit like a psychopath in that way you do
when things are far too funny not to
and it's the way you gave me your wind-up dinosaur
when you foresaw

107

me being lonely
on the two-minute journey
to the shop
and then
here we are again

oh dear

then I know it's too late
to go back to the date
when this was great
in a disposable kind of way

so now when I say *let's keep it open*
I'm kind of hoping
that there'll be enough belief in the way that we feel
maybe one day I'll wake up and know that this is the real deal
but it's not and we both know it
at least not for right now
and neither of us has the power
to make it work
and surprisingly it hurts to know
there'll be a definite end to this

I've found that those
inevitable ends
can be somewhat sticky
it can be kind of tricky
to extract ourselves from each other's lives
when right now we seem to make each other thrive
I can see there can be casualties
from these casual ties

and when you look into my eyes
as we kiss goodbye
I know that none of it was lies
but that this was for now

and that's perfectly alright
I just might miss the way
that we say
goodnight

BBY BLU

I've been in love with you since before we met
I'm drawn to your apologies
and the way you leave the room when you need to cry
you tell me to give you a minute
you'll be alright
you just need to smoke a fag and sort yourself out
but darling
while you take another drag
and your teeth chatter from a shiver on the inside
it's me that's left outside in the cold
you were the first woman I'd ever loved
and you smelt like uncertainty
tall trees
and mumbling

so what can I do but hold you
and light you up with that baby blue clipper
that you own
but I'll keep

like always

I'll keep it safe

you say you're not ready
but you know that when you are
I'll be ready
to warm you up
when your light goes out
I will be an anchor for you
in the storm of your perceived inadequa-seas
and we know that these waters run deep
but I won't let you drown
unless
it's to drown out the sound
that ricochets round the empty space between your heart and
    mine

and continually tells you that you're not good enough
that space is a void
an abyss
an ether
that you float in amongst deathstars and supernovas
and hazy days when you can't leave the bed

when you're not floating beneath the heavens
you've got your head in the sand
but I need my feet on land
I want to fill that space
but I haven't got the grace to stand out in the cold anymore
you sparkle like dewdrops
that glisten under a frazzled sun
and your faux vegetarianism makes you pure magic
to me

you're perfect

the perfect mess
and I want nothing else than for you to see you like I do
but I am cold
and you keep leaving the room

so I'll hold you
and give you my heart
that you own
but I keep

like always

I'll keep it safe

PANCAKES & YOU

I just pressed my nose to the page to smell
if these pages smelt good enough to hold the words that I want
    to write to you
now there is a brown smudge on the page
like the golden tint on your nose
when I give you a kiss

that's not a smudge I'll rub away
and
neither is this

the pages smell quite good
which is annoying in a way

if I believe that these are not the words
then I might trick myself long enough to
write some down

like that

I feel better when you're around

I wrote that in smaller print because I got shy

I tell people you're not funny
all the time
because we've got toes my love
so that we can be kept on them

but the sad truth is
I'm pretty sure
you're the funniest person I've ever met
and when you put my duvet on your back
and call yourself a *big purple bat*
I want to cry at how impossibly *alive* you are

even when you aren't making me happy
you are

you are light
in the dark places

and some day when you feel lonely
I hope you close your eyes
and find your core
and know that I've already climbed inside you
and made a nest with your love

you keep me warm
right at my centre
and shout *eat shit* to all my Dementors
you're pancakes in bed
watching *Friends*
and holding me while I cry
telling me it'll be alright
and that you are mine

you're rolling down hills and stealing Sainsbury's bags
and creating scenes on public transport
you're what's right when I lose
what's left

I know it's confusing that love can manifest
in a multitude of shapes and sometimes
mine can shift into a cube with edges sharp enough
to push you away

I hate that fucking cube

but just like rock cannot beat paper
that cube covered in cobwebs cannot beat you

you're a problem-solving super machine and
better than the person of my dreams because when I wake up
you're still there

forever can't always mean forever
thank you is better than *I love you* sometimes

I am *grateful* for you

you've shown me places in my heart that I didn't know existed
you've made the wounds not hurt so much
you've shown me that a thing like this can live and breathe and
    grow in this world

thank you
you'll always be one of the best friends I ever had
thank you

LUNACY

I know you've captured me
because when I cycle home
I see the small of your back
where the moon should be

LOST FRIENDS

it was a definite risk to love me
the turmoil of those slow years
when I might
and might not have been

and I watched them fall away
dark circles forged by fragility
and the sheer exhaustion that comes
with witnessing
a gutted soul

and they watched me
obliterate
unable to forgive
the obstinate ornaments of self-loathing
I had built
and refused to let rust in the attic

even the most precious stars do fall
and when they cannot return
their absence forces the stark realisation

there is a unique threat that lives buried in the balance
between enduring sickness and enduring love

ELEMENTS

this/ morning
I wasn't ready/ to open my eyes
so I rolled /over
rested my /head on your breast
felt/ your free/ hand
deleting misplaced forward slashes
and hoped you'd understand
that you offer the world
a view from within flames

you'll never know your fire
you're not supposed to

you curate my softest moments

WHEN YOU'RE WHAT I NEED

what is it in me that feels the need to hold you in my branches?
am I feeding from your misery
or is it that you
are
ivy
and without me
standing impenetrable
you would have nothing to cling on to?

18th October – dinner w/ him

she doesn't love **him**
but she cares about **him**
and if she left **him**
it would destroy h**im**
and she cares about **him** too much to destroy **him**

-          something other than love

What Feeds Me?

SUN   HEALTHY MEALS   MY GUITAR
TIME ALONE   PHOTOGRAPHY
NEW HAIR   WRITING   TRAVELLING
DANCING   SEX (JOKING MUM
READING   A BATH   I'VE NEVER HAD
(make time to read!)   ROUTINE   WRITING   SEX - I DON'T EVEN KNOW
AT LEAST   LISTS   HOW TO SPELL
7 HOURS   YOGA   MUM &   INCENSE   JENITALS)
SLEEP   DAD   CYCLING   HOME
GAME   THERAPY
NIGHT   PAINTING   COOKING
REPEATING   MEDITATING
WATCHING TV SERIES   BREATHING

What Feeds You?

MOTHER: WOMB

bury my arrested eyes
in the valley of your chest
wrinkled flesh
your touch holds me under clear dappled waters
willingly
submerged

is this what it was like?
waiting before I met you?

held

amniotic blanket
willingly submerged

FLYING

there's a wall I like to sit on and watch the world go by
but today I sit and sit and sit and sit and sit and wait for you
rectangles for limbs
it seemed like you flew

I met you once before in a very big park in Cardiff
you asked for my number which I found alarming because
    we'd only spoken in poetry
wild poetry under sunlit trees
and at dusk you flew away at light speed
there was somewhere else and someone else you might've
    needed to be
I've only met you once before in a very big park in Cardiff
but I listen to your voice in the mornings before I decide
to glide
reluctantly into another day
and give the world a chance

be brave

I recommend you to my friends and say
I think you are a sweet soul
and now I am waiting for you in a deckchair
in a big jacket I just bought from a charity shop
that makes me feel very cool
and I don't think anyone knows
that I am not

your soul is the perfect sweetness
and if I took a bite
I think I'm right
to think it might taste quite
like a Pink Lady
with the perfect crunch
the best of all the apples

your eyes sing to me in arias and slow jazz

and when I listen for too long I get lost
because really
I don't know you
and I find it confusing
that I'm willingly using this time to wait
and wait
and wait
and wait
for someone I met only once before
in a very big park in Cardiff
I mean maybe I'm hungover
or maybe I'm backpedalling because you just came over
and I don't feel proper

honesty is merciless

I might run back to my wall or the deckchair
and hope that when you don't find me there
you'll know I had to fly
sometimes the sky is safer

but you already knew that

SLOW RISING

you know when you arrange to meet someone on the tube
and you're not quite sure which direction they'll come from
so you're looking in all
seventeen
waiting for a flash of beige
or khaki
you always wear the same coat
I have ten to your one and I like it
I can recognise that coat and trainers a mile away
unless you're wearing your new purple shoes

I'm pretty sure they're blue

my seashells show me pictures of you
I feel like I'm cheating
going down an escalator feels like the opposite of a
rollercoaster

I don't know why they get such good press

surely a slow incline of anticipation is opposed with a slow
decline of disappointment

you arrive somewhere you aren't sure you want to be
lost on the District line

PIKORUA

your skin was glitter
your eyes were a bungalow
I watched you grow
force yourself through
a soil doused in disconnect
to reach my rays
you trusted my warmth
and our love made you into a man

you let yourself cry
and even better
you let yourself smile
and my
what a smile

I drew paintings in your fine hair
found maps amongst your moles
and traced your body
home

darling you can't store love in little holes and keep her there till
    Christmas

what if she dies?
and then
as you wait for her
to rise
you take the time
to realise
that you had lied

your

whole

damn

life

FAIRIES & LIONS

I knew you were a lioness
but I could not have foreseen
that your den would dwell
opposite the Krispy Kreme's
in Victoria station

you tore at the flesh
around my cardiac cavity
with admirable subtlety

I watched your unhappiness trickle like coconut oil down my
    skin
and I wondered if I should warn the cleaner
to put up a sign
so unsuspecting commuters
didn't slip on the run-off

and I wondered if I ran to the guards
watching us on CCTV
and told them there was a patisserie casualty by a Krispy
Kreme's
a self-raising love
tired of pulling itself up
I wondered if they'd display it on the boards
label the trains as delayed
ask all passengers to wait
for three minutes
as this sweet heart breaks

wandering souls like sprinkles
are a lot easier to handle
than hastily burnt edges

we were an unhappy idea
lightly baked fairies
misplaced timing
and rearranged priorities
angular loving

YOU
WERE
THE
BEST
AND
WORST
OF ME

my trauma recognised yours like an avalanche

does that count as passion?
is it understanding what it is to want to rip off your own skin?
is it knowing that these might be the clothes that we die in?
is it spending all night walking along unmarked roads crying?
is it shouting at yourself while driving?
is it

a mountain of stunned words
waiting
as you sing your siren song
waiting
until petrified
my voice calcifies
trapped between unseen tears
and swallowed down deep
with room for doughnuts

did you tell me here so I wouldn't cry?
so you wouldn't have to see me
die a little bit inside

and silently sit on a mountain?

you were a cowardly lion
who scraped out my tin can heart
and plastered over the hole with icing

I deserved more
than a meek end to forever and
your curdled goodbye

how could this be the only poem I ever wrote you?
doesn't that say it all?

A BIT OF WHAT I MEAN WHEN I
SAY THE UNIVERSE

you asked me what it felt like
to make love to you

I closed my eyes
and searched for a way to ask you
how it was possible
that you had met
danced with
and held my whole body
in another time
swaying slowly under moons
transcendent
tender
touches
tearing me through space
I felt warmth from the sun
but refused to be burnt by the rays

I drifted amongst the stars

my skin vibrating in constellations
I breathed in the universe
lost inside the reverberating drum of your heart
pounding me to peace
your chest was my satellite
we'd orbit Saturn's rings
and find

one   single   breath

then

you'd sing

sometimes

you'd sing

we are bigger than the sum of our fears my angel

can't you see?

the cosmos is ours

SCHOOL DAYS

under a towering cavernous wreck
I crawled for days in the velveteen deep
fleeing speech

echoing calls of a name I had never had

it could have been three miles to the whiteboard
dry wipe my way to the next boulder
that I might lean against

tick tock of the socket

forty-eight times
that's twelve times four
which
sat right
at the front of the class
seemed as though
maybe I'd pass the maths exam
and Mum wouldn't crash
head-first
into the windscreen
of her jollof-coloured daydreams

if I could sync the tick tock
of the socket
and
the blur of the ball

                    intercepted

                        mid

                        air

breeze scraped my knees
and I landed
soft cushion of concussion
because no I couldn't make it to
the optician's at the back of Boots

not on my own
without avoiding lines
abacus counting – four times
for my
blurred vision and far-away glimmers
of untainted sight

I wouldn't make it back there
and they wouldn't let me back on the fucking court

since I found a zebra crossing on my arm

I held my breath when I crossed the road
or bridges

because legs have a habit of giving way

black and white like zebras
but
mine were viscous cherries
growing across my arm

SORT OF ALRIGHT

pale drops and nails chipped
on the way to the bottom
of a bottle
that I didn't buy

I'm fine
always
I promise you
just fine

THE CITY

cities swallow me whole
and when I'm chased by pavements
the buildings force themselves apart and make space for me
I cross the barrier
and stand trembling between two shops made of mosaic
I pray
remember how to breathe
and hide
until the last car passes by

WHEN I'M WHAT YOU NEED

you've started to
limit your dosage
decided it might be best to
titrate your experience
into manageable moments
because

you can have too much of a good thing

drops of me
echoing
while you
encapsulate my essence
and turn your face from mine
put distance between our sighing hearts
you lean your head against the door
waiting for this to restore you

but I didn't ask to be medicinal
or to be the one you chose
when to consume
you presumed
I was prescribed
and
I let you

select   extract   discard
my love

I was never meant to be your medicine
but you took me once every three months after a good meal
as if my love was only here to help you heal

EXPECTATIONS

we expect too much
from those
that cannot reason

STORY UPLOADING

you use the word *open*
as if your heart isn't imploding
sleepless nights
married to cheap concealer
hiding
the bags for life under my eyes
pages of a story
I choose to share less often

UNDO

I'm struggling to write about this
because I still don't believe that this is it
girl
I remember repeatedly trying to tell you
that if you took your own life
you'd take mine
and so many others with you
and the day I heard
all I wanted to do
was click

u   n   d   o

undo

undo

and when people asked if I had seen the clues
I look at them blankly
thinking
how can I answer that if you got the nerve to ask me
I'm fucking angry
you weren't a friend
you were like family
and I'm not sure if it's a feasible idea
but I'd move mountains to get you back here
I'm carrying your photos around in my notebook
but there's no need
because you're everywhere I look

but I can't go back
I can't click undo
so I'm still writing just like you'd want me to
I'll never forget you or your love for the spiciest food
I miss you
but I'm still standing here
for you

; THE SEMICOLON MOVEMENT

a semicolon in literature
means another line has been drawn in the picture
sorry
I know that *sounds* like a contradiction
so let me reapply it to fiction

it indicates a sentence that a writer saw as complete

technically
it *could* have been put to an end
but instead they chose the better option
to extend

felt that there was more of the narrative to write
and so in this grammatical symbol
thousands of people have chosen to unite

because you see
we are the authors
and our lives are that sentence
every day that we live
we have chosen not to end it

and maybe
that doesn't mean much to you
could sound a little bit glib
why compare on and off
to the manoeuvre of a dimmer switch?

I'll tell you why I write lines
on this element of punctuation
because someone I hold close
was in a very different situation

I never knew there was such finality
in the filling of a stop
but I assure you

once that stop is full
it can't contain another drop
there's no more ink on that page
no plot twists or predictable writing
there's just the silence of a voice
that was too tired to keep fighting

maybe it's hard to relate
so let's open another gate
we can stumble down a cobbled path
and look at faces that'll hide
their tears with a forced laugh

would you do something for me?
would you bring someone you love to mind?
someone who is of a bizarre but undeniably brilliant kind
and then think of a time you've seen in a very real way
them struggle on through
a hollow shell of a day
and because their mind is a fortress
made of solid fortified wood
you can't see what they're thinking
don't know if you'd want to if you could

so the only thing you can do
is believe not much is at stake
that they've not been spending the last four years
trying not to break

to shatter like fragments
of a glass that was always half-full
jarringly unmarked fragments
near-infinitesimal
now we go back to the point
and I'm not talking the decimal

think of that person

see their annoyingly great smile
then envisage they weren't going to be around for a while

I know it's unpleasant and it's grim
but it is a damning reality
that sometimes
this little life
can meet an unexpected finality

so I appreciate the semicolon
that blessed piece of punctuation
and the unbelievably important value
in an author's choice
of
continuation

HEARTSONG

there are some that will sing the songs your heart forgets
with perfect pitch
refusing to leave out the minors
seeing how darkness makes you rich
and though they are just as lost as you
they will hold you while they sing
crafting a nest with their voice that illuminates
darkness isn't how your melody ends

AUTUMN

prisms gather in puddles
colours huddle
between
crushed leaves
I breathe in

draw the curtains tight

then my eyes

and wait for spring again

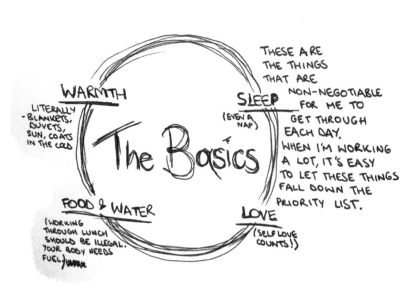

WARMTH

LITERALLY
- BLANKETS,
DUVETS,
SUN, COATS
IN THE COLD

The Basics

SLEEP

(EVEN A
NAP)

THESE ARE
THE THINGS
THAT ARE
NON-NEGOTIABLE
FOR ME TO
GET THROUGH
EACH DAY.
WHEN I'M WORKING
A LOT, IT'S EASY
TO LET THESE THINGS
FALL DOWN THE
PRIORITY LIST.

FOOD & WATER

(WORKING
THROUGH LUNCH
SHOULD BE ILLEGAL.
YOUR BODY NEEDS
FUEL)

LOVE

(SELF LOVE
COUNTS!)

THE QUESTION

it started with a question
someone asked me

what was it like?

and I shrugged and said
it was okay
because in all honesty
I didn't know what to say
I looked in his eyes and wondered if really
there was a way for me to explain clearly
what it was like
did he really want to know?
or was it all for show?
just to prove that he cared
when people stared
because I burst out crying
when my travel card didn't work

the question

when the answer is an unknown it feels quite fine
to spill all your guts out on the yellow line
to detail all the heartache and the woe
if he really wants to know
but does he really want to know?
what it's like
well for me
and I can only speak for me
and not the 350 million people globally
suffering from this disease
well technically it's an illness
but rhyming is hard so
let's not split hairs

what was it like?

it felt like someone took a melon scoop

and went down my insides
until there was nothing left
I was completely bereft
of hope
I felt alone
like nowhere could ever be home
I felt like I was in the bottom of a hole
and it was getting really fucking cold
and no matter how hard I screamed
no one could hear my pleas
I felt like I'd lost a part of me that I never knew was there
and along with that the ability to care
I felt like shit

but that was me

and there's another side of this you see
I guess you've also got to think about what it's like to hear
that someone that you hold very dear
feels broken inside
that they just want to hide
I can see
and have seen
both sides
of what it's like

and I know you might not know what to say
but I am shouting out loud
that this is all kinds of okay
because to be clear
your question
might save a life one day
not necessarily

what is it like?

but maybe

how are you?
are you alright?

are you really alright?
or even   *do you think you might... need help?*

you might not want to know what it's like
but until we educate lovers and brothers
children will continue to grow up and
fall through the cracks
because of the devastating lack
of funding
from a system that is at breaking point

cuts

yes cuts in wrists
end lives
but cuts in funding also
end lives
and I suppose I strive
to get people talking
even at eight o'clock in the morning
when you're walking to a class
and your friend says they can't be arsed
because they're feeling
just a bit low
give it a go
because I lied
no one asked the question
no one wanted to know what it's like

ask the question

I promise
it won't give you indigestion
it won't give you a bladder infection
and it probably won't impact the next election
but I think it's time to talk
ask the question

THE WAITING ROOM

all I can do is write to you

I attempted to call your phone the other day
it was disconnected
I hoped I'd hear the *I don't CARE* tone in
your voice
but instead it said

the number you have dialled has not been recognised

so then I tried
to leave you a message anyway
otherwise

you wouldn't know I'd called

but it wouldn't let me

all I can do is write to you
this time I hope you reply

and I don't blame you
it can be fucking hard to bear being here
sometimes
it's clear
we're fighting a war
and the generals have gone out the back door
and we are stranded standing on the battlefield
with trembling fingertips grasping at ghosts for weapons
freezing in our underwear
and underwear feels best at warmer temperatures

we both know that

but I just wish you hadn't left me here
I don't blame you for leaving
but I wish you hadn't

and I'm sitting in this waiting room with a Joni Mitchell song
that won't stop playing
and all the blinds have been shut

so I can't see who else is in here

but I'm not leaving
in case your name
gets called

or mine

but the air is starting to get stale
and the voice on the tannoy doesn't sound so nice
no matter how hard I try I cannot imagine that voice having
kind eyes

I really want the voice that calls your name to be **kind**

and I'm sitting on this threadbare chair
    and I'm *picking* at the foam
roaming around a darkened room
    wondering if they keep magazines
in this
in-between
wondering why thoughts of magazines
    creep inside my mind like insects
insp-sp-sp-specting
where to find me idle
    because I don't even read magazines

           we both know that

actually
I think I'll check again
I might have got the timing wrong

I mean
the lyrics of this song are
quite offbeat
and surely when your name is called
there should be pure

s y n c h r o n i c i t y

I need to go to the toilet
but I don't want to lose my place
so I wonder if I pisssssssed on the seat
if they'd turn on the lights
and then maybe that unkind voice on the tannoy would say

*I'm sorry
but this isn't right
you're in the wrong room*

and ask me to leave
because the smell was unbearable
the brutal mix of anticipation and

urine

but I can't
stop
waiting

I don't know how

listen my girl
I've still got all your art
and I just don't understand why the world won't get to see it
and you need to tell me what your secret language meant
because I've got all these notes you left me

and I don't know what they say

and this room smells of cigarettes and

depression

earlier I stared at some scaffolding out of the window for ten
minutes
because it had a bag attached to it
and the bag was moving in the wind
and because I can't move at all

I'm suffocating in the stench and fear of forgotten faces
lingering in this
otherwise

I feel like things would all make sense if
you
were
here
but I know that's not true either

we'd just be lost together
would that life be better?

and I know one day I'll read this at a poetry night
and I'll cry
and people might feel sad
because that's a thing to do

and I'll hate myself for it
for turning it into a poem that I read in a room with people
who don't know who you were
and who won't know whether it's appropriate
to clap

because what I really want to do is

throw these words on the floor
and scream at the sky
and tell the gods
THAT ALL OF THIS IS WRONG
and that
YOU SHOULDN'T HAVE GONE

but I probably won't do that

because I don't know if I'm right

I don't know

I don't know if you can hear this
and I don't know if you're at peace
I don't know if you're laughing because Trump is president
and you would have found our liberal optimism hilarious
I don't know if your coriander dip is still as hot as it was
or if you're making it for an angel

or if I believe in angels
or if I believe in stolen lyrics
or stolen moments
or if I believe in

KALI

she found you
suspended in the darkness
immobilised in suffering
devoid of space and time

she whispered
let today be new
make something of
this vast nothing
you've done it before
and you will do it again

she keened
let the light in
this is not a home divine enough for you
log the **truth**
you are undeniably good

she exhaled
let today be new
abolish yesterday
wash away tomorrow
figments are but fragments
my friend
and now is all there is

she found you
absolutely surrendered to chaos
with mildewed boundaries
and a blissful lack of responsibility

and she persisted

please
let the light in
today came when you wholeheartedly believed that
it would not

don't you owe it that?

CAROLINE

I don't know how to make things better
when I open an eye
I can see you squashed
raw fingers
tapping
glass
gasping for space
to breathe
my heart gravitates towards yours
but I hide
I hide
because
I'm squashed too
my face is pressed against you
and they've left us so little light that you can't see me
my heart gravitates towards yours
and I'm crying on the District line because I don't know how to
help
this world is built for me to watch the ones I love
burning
and I don't know how to help

INVISIBLE

they cannot see it
they cannot see it
they cannot see it

and sometimes I wish we turned   blue

so that everytime we walked in
offbeat
slow motion
without explanation
they'd understand
that there are bandages
they cannot see
wrapped around our hearts

SPOONS

there was magic in her fingertips

when she called out to the universe
it reached back with armoured roots
to wrap around her feet
tethered her like kite strings

so she could fly
without burning
weathered wings

so she could cry
with her best friend
by a sun lamp
melting into duvets

she rebuilt her wings
with borrowed tools
she found fuel for the day
with borrowed spoons
and when they asked
how she did it all
she said
it was all that
damn
magic
in her fingertips

MUSCLE MEMORY

there are memories
with legs
that know how to chase
that have discovered how to survive
in inhospitable environments
that have learnt to endure
what
you
cannot
there are memories with legs
that search for you

legs
that you would rather break

than touch

ALONE AT THE FEAST

if the one that grows is the one you feed
why do I starve myself
smiling at your banquet
from behind my empty plate?

CHASING WARMTH

why doesn't simple pulsating joy
fascinate me
unless I've forgotten and then remembered
how to believe in it?
the curse and blessing in forgetting

COMPANY

I stole your soul on the Underground
and took it with me on the commute
it got me through conversations
about what is 'big' right now
and
how tired we all were
your soul made it look like I cared

the heart's
memory
eliminates
the bad and
magnifies the
good and that
wants to this
before we
manage to
endure the
burden of
the
past...

THE GREATEST EXPECTATION

I pity all of those versions of me
frozen by the belief that they

**should
be
doing
better**

you are here little one

the universe expects nothing from you
your birth and your death are inevitable

to live
is the choice

LITTLE THANKS

Cashauna, Chloë, Rhian, Kate, DHG, Tyler, Julie, Gareth, Janette, Mike, Gail, Fuschia, Colin, Daffodil, Nick, Divya, Mama Harvey, Hannah, Mama Beth, Caroline, Ava, Maddy, Sammy, Leander, Alex, Tim, Zara, Dan, Emma, Sophia, Amy, Tanusha, ArtsEd, the NHS, West London Rape Crisis, Burning Eye Books.

Sofa. For confronting me with the ugly truth of in sickness *and* in health.

Ebere. For, since infancy, fiercely forcing me to understand the beauty in being black.

Umuanunu Nsu, Nigeria. For the gift of roots.

My family. For **everything**.

You. For making it this far.

And lastly Jack, my angel, my dearest friend, thank you. For always finding my wandering, tired and lost little turtle heart. And bringing it home.

Cover Design by Judith P. Raynault

Illustration Credits

Rachel Nwokoro
Divya Scialo
Chloë Lund
Rhian Morris
Bethany Rose
Caroline Teague
Zara Daswani
Anand Sagar
Ava Pickett
Hannah Harvey
Ijeoma Nwanesi

BUSINESS BITS

Rachel Nwokoro is a young black woman of Nigerian heritage, specifically belonging to the Indigenous people of Biafra.

And she loves telling stories.

Earlier in her career, as she explored acting, directing and writing, she felt uncomfortable with the pressure put on her by the arts industry to choose a single path and specialise. It echoed the narrow-eyed representation she found of herself in popular culture. She then realised that she alone had the power to reclaim and shape her own narrative through art.

Rachel is dedicated to experimenting across diverse disciplines in order to discover the awkward, irregular and miraculous shapes that hide within our stories.

We are uncontainable creatures.

Rachel likes colouring out of the lines.

Although Rachel has been performing spoken word poetry for four years (nationally and internationally), she has been telling stories for much longer. She has worked professionally as an actor since the age of thirteen after knocking on agents' doors, subsequently getting signed and only alerting her parents after the event. Never one to take the path well-travelled, some years later, Rachel was awarded the Vice Chancellor's Scholarship for the Arts at Durham University, where she read a BSc in Natural Sciences (Biology, English and French) for two years while directing multiple productions.

In August 2018, Rachel directed sell-out show *Funeral Flowers* at Edinburgh Fringe Festival. She is currently in her final year of training with a full scholarship at acclaimed drama school Arts Educational Schools London.

In the past she has worked with the RSC, Royal Court, Soho Theatre, Lyric Theatre, Her Majesty's Theatre, Actors Centre, ITV, Nationwide, Sky News, NSPCC, Nickelodeon, Birmingham Opera Company, Saatchi & Saatchi, Fortnum & Mason, Tricycle Theatre, Thames Festival Trust – Resident Poet, Roundhouse – Resident Artist, Circuito Nacional Poetry Slam MX – Resident

Poet in Mexico, La Coupe du Monde – Paris, Spoken Word Paris, Stonewall UK, Sofar Sounds, Shambala Festival, Brainchild Festival and many other renowned organisations worldwide.

Rachel has also won a number of awards and competitions, most notably 2016 UK Slam Poetry Champion.

She wants to help make the world better.

www.rachelshapes.com
@RachelShapes

Lightning Source UK Ltd.
Milton Keynes UK
UKHW021907130519
342588UK00008B/41/P